Reykjavík, Iceland

, Hallfreði "Hadda" Lárussyni

Iceland

as made possible through the help and assistance of
nd the book's photographic subject, Friðrik Örn Sigþórsson;
her, Sigþór "Siggi" Hallfreðsson and Erla Friðriksdóttir;
ðrik Jónsson and the *Gauti*;
llfreður "Haddi" Lárusson and the *Inga*;
var "Elli" Halldór Hallfreðsson and Lárus "Lolli" Franz Hallfreðsson;
the director of the Iceland Tourist Board in New York;
he manager of communications and media relations for Icelandair.

ere taken during the summer of 2002 in Reykjavík, Stykkishólmur, and coastal Iceland,
F23 with 24-, 85-, 105 micro-, 180-, and 300-millimeter lenses.
as often used when shooting in full sunlight.
m, Kodachrome 64, was processed by Kodak at Fair Lawn, New Jersey.

be found at www.brucemcmillan.com.

Cataloging-in-Publication Data

and photo-illustrated by Bruce McMillan.

s."

Juvenile literature. I. Title.

2

                    2004015506

201-7

3 2 1

an
Caxton.

Going Fishi

written and photo-illus

Bruce McM

Houghton Mifflin Compar

Walter Lorraine

Tileinkuð

Going Fishing v
my young friend
his father and mo
his grandfather Fr
his grandfather Ha
Siggi's brothers, E
Einar Gústavsson,
and Debbie Scott, t

The photographs w
using a Nikon F4/N
A polarizing filter v
The 35-millimeter fi

More information ca

Walter Lorraine

Library of Congress

McMillan, Bruce.
Going fishing / writte
p. cm.
"Walter Lorraine book
ISBN 0-618-47201-0
1. Fishing—Iceland—
SH643.I25M39 2005
799.16'09163'24—dc

ISBN-13: 978-0-618-47

Printed in Singapore
TWP 10 9 8 7 6 5 4

Designed by Bruce McMill
The text is set in 11-point

"Don't forget your hat," said his mother. But Friðrik *(FREEDTH • rik)* didn't need it. He was in a hurry to get to the pósturinn *(POST • uhr • in)*, the post office, near his home. He lived in the city of Reykjavík *(RAYK • yah • veek)*, Iceland. Friðrik lived in the land of fish.

Friðrik spent his money, coins faced with cod and lumpfish. He bought some stamps printed with cod and lumpfish. He had two letters to mail, one for each of his grandfathers. They lived in Stykkishólmur *(STICK • ee • shohl • mur)*. Friðrik had written back to them about next week.

One of his grandfathers was a doctor and the other a school custodian. In the summer, they were both fishermen. One caught cod. The other caught lumpfish. Friðrik was going fishing.

Early one evening the following week, Friðrik arrived in the tiny fishing village of Stykkishólmur.

"Tomorrow we're going fishing," said his mother's father. It was Grandfather Friðrik, the doctor, for whom young Friðrik was named. "Just as the young terns are learning to fish, tomorrow you'll come fishing with me. But we're going fishing for cod. We'll leave early. Be ready, and remember what your mother always says."

"I know. Don't forget my hat," Friðrik said, and they laughed together.

He didn't. Friðrik had on his húfa *(HOO • vah)*, a traditional Icelandic hat made by his grandmother just for him. He also had on his jacket with built-in flotation, a life jacket.

Once aboard the *Gauti (GOW • tee)*, the two Friðriks sped out to the fishing grounds. The *Gauti* was fast.

His grandfather said, "Steer in this direction, Friðrik," and pointed to a setting on the compass. His grandfather knew just where to go. He had been fishing here for years.

Twenty minutes later his grandfather slowed the engine to an idle. As they drifted, he pointed to the depth finder. There was some movement on the screen. "That might be some codfish swimming under us," he said.

"But I didn't bring my fishing rod," replied young Friðrik. "You said I wouldn't need it."

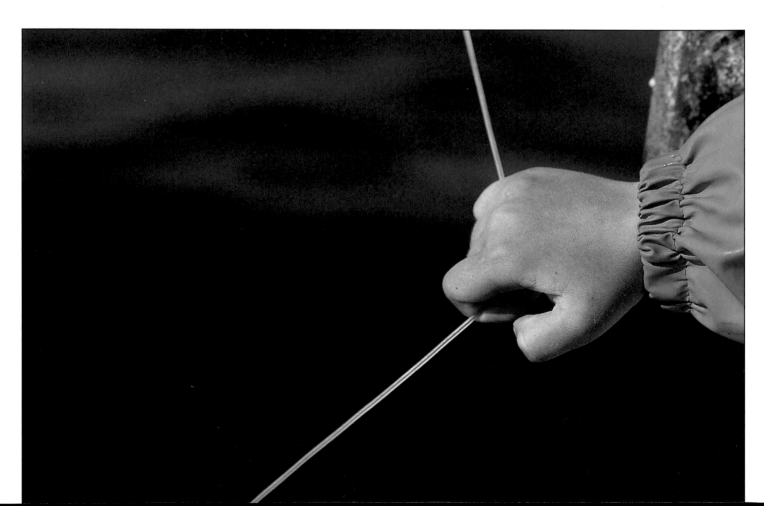

"That's right," said his grandfather. "We don't need rods because the reels are built right onto the boat. We don't even need live bait. The lures are already on the hooks. They look like worms."

Once the line was out it was young Friðrik's job to jig for fish. He gave the line three quick tugs. He did it again and again. Soon he felt the line tugging back.

"I feel something," said young Friðrik. "It's a fish!"

"Well then, reel it in," said his grandfather, and he did.

It looked like a big fish to young Friðrik. But his grandfather said, "Oh, it's just a tiny codfish. And there's only one."

All along the end of the line were many hooks and lures, but only one hook had a fish. His grandfather carefully took the hook out of the fish's mouth. He handed the small fish to young Friðrik and said, "We'll catch this one again when he's bigger."

As the *Gauti* rolled in the swells, young Friðrik dropped the fish back into the sea. They played out the line once again.

Soon young Friðrik exclaimed, "I have a big one, a really big one! I can feel it."

13

"This one's a keeper," grunted young Friðrik. It was a struggle just to hold the heavy, slippery fish. On this line they caught more than one cod. Most of them were keepers.

"See the little whisker under the chin?" asked his grandfather. "It's a barbel. That's how you can tell it's a cod. It's as if they have their tongues hanging out. It has taste buds, like your tongue."

The fish bin was half full when the wind picked up. As they bobbed on the swells, his grandfather swung the boat around. "Time to head back to port," said his grandfather. "Your father's waiting for us."

On the ride back he passed young Friðrik a snack he had brought along for them—dried codfish. It was a fitting way to end their trip.

That evening Friðrik and his father, Siggi *(SIG • ee)*, hiked up to the lighthouse.

His father said, "Tomorrow, I'm going fishing with you. We're going with my father, Grandfather Haddi [*HAD • ee*]. I used to work on his boat when I was a boy."

"Are there lines with hooks for both of us?" asked Friðrik.

"We won't be catching the fish with hooks. We'll be catching them with nets. But we'll use a hook to free the fish from the nets. The nets are already set for the fish. We'll be going out to haul them early in the morning. By the way, you know what your mother told me to tell you?"

"I know, I know. Don't forget my hat."

The next morning Friðrik didn't forget his hat. But he didn't need it once he was inside the cabin.

Friðrik was busy steering the boat. Haddi was helping him. Friðrik's father was getting things ready outside. The *Inga* chug-chugged along. It was a very slow fishing boat, and it took more than an hour to reach the nets.

As they got closer, Haddi pointed to the horizon and said, "We want to head for that island."

Friðrik kept the *Inga* on course. Soon he saw something between them and the island.

"What's that?" asked Friðrik.

"That's the net buoy. It's tied to the first net we're going to haul today. Better put on your hat. It's time to see if we've caught any lumpfish."

Under water, the net hung like a straight curtain. The fish got caught in the holes of the netting. One end of the hanging net was attached to the buoy. As they pulled alongside the buoy, Friðrik reached out and grabbed it. His grandfather wrapped the net's lines around the winch. Friðrik stared at the net coming up, trying to see his first lumpfish.

"We've caught one!" announced Friðrik. "What an ugly fish!"

As the net slid down the table chute, it was Friðrik's job to pull out the biggest pieces of seaweed. Overboard they went. He spotted a small lumpfish.

"That little lumpfish is a boy," said Grandfather Haddi.

"How do you know?" asked Friðrik.

"The lumpfish girls are always big and the boys are always small. Turn him over and you can see something else. See the sucker under his chin? All lumpfish have one. They use it to hold on to the ocean bottom when the current is strong. You can toss him overboard, Friðrik. We're keeping only the females today."

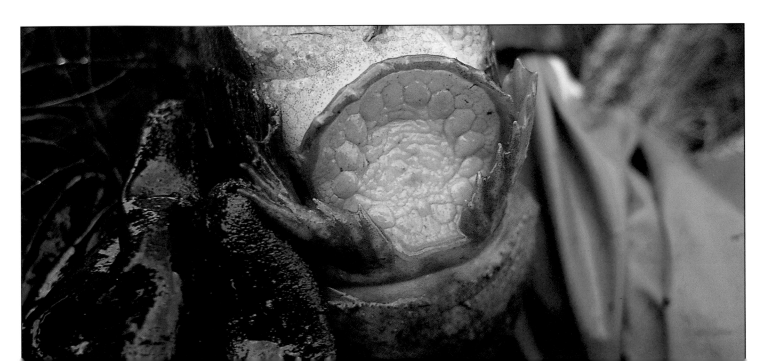

Everyone had a job. His grandfather hauled the nets and steered the boat. It was Friðrik's job to pull away the netting and free the fish. He used a hook to do it. Then he passed the female fish to his father. Siggi's job was to clean the fish. He also piled up the net so that it was ready to drop back overboard. There was one thing left to do. That job would soon be Friðrik's.

All morning long they went from island to island, net to net. They kept the female fish, not because they were big, but because of what was inside of them.

They were fishing for the eggs, the roe. In early summer the female lumpfish were full of eggs. This was the only part of the fish that was usually sold. Some of the fishermen traditionally ate the meat of the males, but they all made their living from selling the roe.

"Can I feel it?" asked Friðrik, and his father passed some to him. "It feels like lumpy jelly."

His father replied, "But it tastes like fish eggs. Hey, look at your face. You're covered in seaweed. You look like a working fisherman. Turn around and you'll see the friends of the fishermen."

Friðrik turned to see all the birds. They always followed the fishing boats and helped clean up.

The fish eggs were the catch, so the rest of the fish scraps were fed to the birds. While his father was cleaning fish and his grandfather was tending to the nets, Friðrik made lots of friends. This was Friðrik's favorite job, feeding the fish scraps to the birds.

Grandfather Haddi said, "They look like seagulls, don't they, Friðrik? They aren't. There's a tube on the top of their nose. These birds are fulmars. Their name comes from an old Icelandic name *fúlmár,* meaning 'foul gull.' They spray vomit at you if you bother them on their nests. It smells awful."

"Good thing we're not bothering them," said Friðrik as he continued feeding the birds.

Finally, all the fishing nets, except one that needed mending, were back in the sea. The fish-egg barrels were full and the fulmars all fed. It was time to head back to shore.

Friðrik helped wash down the decks. The weary fisherman watched the islands fade into the horizon.

Once ashore, his grandfather said, "Friðrik, aren't you forgetting something?"

"What?" asked Friðrik.

"Don't forget your hat," said Haddi as he put his own hat on Friðrik. "Now you're a fisherman."